Tellin

Short stories retold by

Fiona Collins

**'When the storyteller speaks,
the sun and the clouds stop to listen.'**

Nelson

Thomas Nelson and Sons Ltd
Nelson House Mayfield Road
Walton-on-Thames Surrey
KT12 5PL UK

Nelson Blackie
Wester Cleddens Road
Bishopbriggs
Glasgow
G64 2NZ UK

Thomas Nelson Australia
102 Dodds Street
South Melbourne
Victoria 3205 Australia

Nelson Canada
1120 Birchmount Road
Scarborough Ontario
MIK 5G4 Canada

Illustrated by David Bez, Jill Newton

First published by Thomas Nelson and Sons Ltd 1996
I(T)P Thomas Nelson is an International Thomson Publishing Company
I(T)P is used under licence

ISBN 0-17-401290-X

Printed in China

Contents

Introduction

A story, a story,
Let it come, let it go.

Stories have been in the world for a long, long time. As long as there have been human beings, there have been stories.

There were stories before there were books, and many of the stories in books were first told by storytellers long ago. Today there are many storytellers all around the world, telling stories, jokes and riddles to people who love to listen.

The stories in this book come from some of these storytellers. You will find stories from different countries, and also riddles and rhymes at the beginning and end of the stories. If you like them, you can use them when you tell stories! They are for sharing, and telling, and passing on.

One storyteller from Scotland says, 'A story is the best kind of present, because when you give it to someone, you can still keep it for yourself.'

I think he is right! Share these stories, keep these stories, and *enjoy* them.

Do you know what else the storytellers say?

'Three apples fell from the sky;
One for the one who told the story,
One for the one who heard the story,
And one for the one who understood.'

How the sun came

A Native American legend

Long, long ago, before there were any people in the world, only the animals, it was dark all the time.

Dark in the night time and dark in the day time.

Dark in the day time and dark in the night time.

And life was hard for the animals. They couldn't see to find their food. They couldn't see where they were going. They had bumps and cuts and bruises because they were always falling down in the dark. They were thin because they couldn't find any food.

Now Coyote was a clever animal. He was full of tricks. He got tired of falling down. He got tired of being thin. He said to himself, 'If I had a friend to help me, life would not be so hard. Who shall

I choose to be my friend?'

He looked all around and he chose Eagle – Eagle with her sharp claws, her strong beak, her powerful wings. He went to Eagle and he said, 'Let's be friends. We can do everything together and life will be easier for us both.'

So Coyote and Eagle became friends and they helped each other to find food, to find somewhere safe to sleep, to find safe places to go. And life was easier for them both.

Then they began to hear stories that far away, in the West, where the

Kachinas lived, there was a bright light which belonged to the Kachinas.

'If only we had that light,' said Coyote, 'We could use it to help us find our way.'

So they decided to travel to the West to find the bright light. They travelled and they travelled for a long time, Coyote walking and Eagle flying, across the long flat grasslands of the world. And sometimes they would see a bright light flash in the sky in the West, and then they would look at each other and nod, because they knew that they could see the light they wanted to find.

At last the long flat grasslands came to an end, and the mountains of the West made a high wall in front of Coyote and Eagle. Now they could see the bright light more and more. They knew they were coming to the end of their journey.

They began to climb the foothills of the mountains. They peeped carefully over some rocks. In front of them they saw the camp of the Kachinas, with their lodges in a circle round the fire. The Kachinas were dancing round the fire and the drummers were drumming. Next to the drummers stood a big wooden box. Coyote and Eagle saw one of the dancers come out of the circle, dance to the box and open it. A bright light shone out. Then the lid of

the box dropped down again and the light was gone. Coyote and Eagle looked at each other. This was the bright light they had come to find!

They watched the dancers and the drummers for a long time. They saw the dancers stop dancing one by one, and yawn, and go into the lodges to sleep. They saw the drummers stop drumming and put down their drums and go into the lodges to sleep. They saw the bright fire burn down until there were only grey ashes and a thin line of smoke. They waited and watched, watched and waited for a long time. At last, when they were sure that everyone was

asleep, they crept over the rocks, they came down the hill, they tiptoed between the lodges and they stepped passed the fire. They picked up the box. Coyote took one side in his strong jaws and Eagle took the other side in her strong claws. Then they carried it, one walking, one

flying, passed the fire, between the lodges, up the hill and down the other side, and away across the long flat grasslands of the world.

They went on for a long time, until Coyote's jaws were sore and Eagle's claws were tired.

Then Coyote said, 'I'm so tired. I want to rest.'

Eagle looked back and said, 'Now I think it is safe to rest. We have walked far enough. The Kachinas will not be able to see us. But we must keep watch in case they wake up and come after us. You can sleep first and I will keep watch.

Then when you have had a rest I will sleep and you can keep watch.'

So Coyote put his nose on his paws and lay down and went to sleep. And Eagle flew up above him into the sky and circled round and round and round, keeping watch. She flew and she flew until her wings were tired and she could not fly any more. Then she flew back down and woke up Coyote.

'Now it's your turn to watch so that I can sleep,' she said to Coyote. Eagle put her head under her wing and went to sleep, and Coyote sat up to watch.

Coyote looked to the East, and he looked to the West, and he looked at the box.

Then he looked to the West, and he looked to the East, and he looked at the box.

He looked to the East, and he looked at the box.

He looked to the West, and he looked

at the box.

He looked at the box and he looked at the box and he looked at the box!

'I wonder what the bright light is like? I just want to have a little peep,' thought Coyote. And he just could not help himself. He had to see! He pushed the lid of the box with his long nose. The lid opened a crack. The bright light came shining out through the crack. But it wasn't just bright, it was hot as well, and it burnt the soft spot at the end of Coyote's nose. He yelped, and jumped back. And when he jumped back his nose bumped on the lid of the box. And when it was bumped the lid of the box opened. And when the lid opened the bright light flew out of the box and up into

the sky – up and up and up!

I don't know what woke up the Eagle –

maybe it was the noise that Coyote made. Maybe it was the bright light shining down from the sky. But she did wake up. And she looked around. She saw Coyote rubbing his burnt nose, she saw the open lid of the box, she saw the bright light up in the sky. Quickly she flapped her wings and flew up into the sky, up and up and up, chasing the bright light. But the bright light went so fast and so high that she could not catch it, and at last she had to come slowly back down again.

Coyote looked at Eagle. Was she cross because Coyote had

opened the box and lost the light? But when Eagle looked at Coyote and saw his worried face, and his burnt nose, she couldn't be cross.

She said, 'Never mind, Coyote. We can't keep the bright light for ourselves, but now that it is in the sky we can share it with all the animals.'

So the bright light stayed up in the sky and made the day time light. The animals could see now to find their food, and to see where they were going. So they were happy.

And if you look up in the sky, you will see that the bright light is still there, even today! And that is the story that the Native American people tell about how the sun came in the sky.

When the story ends, the storyteller says, 'Wire bend, story end.'

What is dark, but made with light?

A shadow

The cat's drum

A creation story from India

In the old, old, long ago days all the animals played the drum. It was good when they had a party because there was always music to dance to.

Some animals played drums that you hit with a stick.

Some animals played drums that you beat with your hands.

Some animals played drums that you shake.

And the cat had a special drum which she played by sliding her paw along the top of the drum from the front to the back. It made a lovely sound.

But there was one animal who didn't have a drum to play. It was the rat. He was very angry because he wanted a drum. He liked the cat's drum very much. He decided to steal the cat's drum for himself and keep it for ever.

Soon the animals had a party. They didn't invite the rat because he had no drum to play. He wasn't at the party. But he was watching the fun. The animals danced and drummed for so long that at last they fell asleep. The cat was asleep in the corner, with her drum under her paw.

But the rat was not asleep.

He was still watching. He crept up to the cat and stole her drum while she was sleeping. Then he ran away as fast as he could. But the cat woke up. She heard him run. She saw her drum was gone. She got mad! She hissed and spat. She put out her claws. She fluffed up her tail. She ran after the rat.

The rat saw her coming, but he kept on running.

He heard her hissing, but he kept on running.

She was getting nearer. He kept on

running.

He ran down a little road. She came after him.

When he got near the end of the road he saw a high wall. He couldn't go over it. He couldn't go under it. He couldn't go round it.

The cat kept coming after him. He had to stop.

He turned round with his back against the wall. He held the drum tight. The cat kept coming. She looked terrible. Her face was fierce. Her eyes were angry.

Her teeth were sharp.

She shouted at him, 'Give me back my drum! Give me back my drum! Give me back my drum!'

He was afraid. He knew she could kill him.

He shouted back to her, 'All right, you can have your silly drum back. I don't care. Only leave me alone!'

And he threw the drum at her. But the cat didn't see. She was too angry. And she didn't hear. She was shouting too loudly. And her mouth was wide, wide, wide open as she shouted.

The rat threw the drum. It flew straight at the cat's face. It flew straight in the cat's mouth ... and she swallowed it!

She stopped shouting and

running. She had a funny look on her face. The rat ran away quickly and hid from her – and even today rat still hides from the cat, because he knows that she is still angry with him.

But the cat has still got her drum, even today. And you can still play it by sliding your hand along the top of the drum. But the drum is inside the cat's

tummy, so you must slide your hand along her back, from her head to her tail.

And when you do that, you will hear the lovely sound of the drum inside her tummy, even today!

These words come from
me to you.
Be they lies or be they
true?

Stretched skin on curved wood,
Beat it hard, it sounds good.

A drum

Riverturtle is not singing

A trickster tale from Mexico

When children are small, their parents tell them things to keep them safe. They say things like, 'Don't go in the road. Don't talk to strangers. Don't run down the stairs.' Did your parents say things like this to you when you were little?

When Riverturtles are small, do you know what their parents say to them to keep them safe?

'Don't go far from the water. Don't go far from the water.'

Turtles can live in the water and on the land, but if they go too far from the water, their skin will get dry, their shells will get cracked, their throats will be dry, and they might even die.

This is the story of a Riverturtle who forgot to listen to what his parents told him!

One day, early in the morning while it was still cool, when the fresh dew was still on the grass and the sun was still low down in the sky, a little Riverturtle came up out of the water and began to

walk along beside the river. He was very happy. He was singing a little turtle song to himself, and thinking his little turtle thoughts. He was so busy singing and thinking that he didn't even notice when the path he was walking along began to go away from the river, and instead of walking on the grass he was walking on the stones. And then instead of walking on the stones he was walking on the rock. And then instead of walking on the rock he was walking on the sand. He was walking out into the desert!

At last he did stop singing and thinking, and he looked around him. All he could see was the hot desert sand. And when he looked up, the burning sun was high in the sky and it was beating down on him. His skin was dry, and his shell felt cracked, and his throat was dry and sore. And when he looked for the river, it was so far away that it just looked like a little blue ribbon away behind him. He was afraid. He might even die!

He didn't know what to do. Then he saw a little hole under some rocks.

'I'll go in there to get out of the hot sun,' he thought. So he crawled under the rocks. Then he looked out. All he could see was the hot desert sand.

How was he going to get home? He was so frightened that he began to cry. Two big turtle tears splashed onto his little turtle feet. When he saw that, he cried more and more. He was crying and crying in the little hole in the rocks.

And while he was crying and crying, who came walking across the desert? It was Coyote, the clever one, the trickster one. And he stopped and listened to the sound.

'Who is singing that lovely song?' asked the Coyote. 'I want to learn that song.'

He came to the little hole under the rocks where the Riverturtle was crying.

'Teach me the song you are singing,' said

Coyote. 'Teach me the song.'

But the Riverturtle said: 'I'm not singing, I'm crying.'

Coyote said: 'If you don't teach me the song that you're singing, I'll push my

long nose in there and I'll pull you right out, and throw you onto the hot desert sand to die!'

So the Riverturtle said, 'I don't care if you push your long nose in here and pull me right out, and throw me onto the hot desert sand to die,

I'm not singing, I'm crying!'

Then Coyote said: 'If you don't teach me the song that you're singing, I'll push my long nose in there and I'll pull you

right out, and throw you into the cactus so all the prickles will go in your bottom!'

So the Riverturtle said, 'I don't care if you push your long nose in here and pull me right out, and throw me into the cactus so all the prickles go in my bottom, I'm not singing, I'm crying!'

Then Coyote said: 'If you don't teach me the song that you're singing, I'll push my long nose in there and I'll pull you right out, and I'll run with you down to the river and I'll throw you into the water to drown!'

And the Riverturtle said, 'Oh, please, please don't throw me into the river to drown!'

So Coyote said, 'If that's what you're afraid of, then that's what I will do!'

So he pushed his long nose under the rocks and he pulled the Riverturtle right out, and he carried him in his mouth and he ran with him –

gallopa-gallopa, over the sand
gallopa-gallopa, over the rock
gallopa-gallopa, over the stones
gallopa-gallopa, over the grass,
until he came to the side of the river. And then he put back his head and he *thr - - - ew* that Riverturtle into the air.

And the Riverturtle flew up in the air and down into the river with a big splash! As he sank down below the water, the cool fresh water soothed his dry skin. And it washed away the cracks in his shell. And he drank and drank until his throat wasn't dry any more.

Then he swam

back to the top and popped his head out of the water. Coyote was still sitting on the riverbank.

‘Thank you, Mr. Coyote, for bringing me home,’ called the Riverturtle. ‘And by the way, I wasn’t singing. I was crying!’

And then he turned round and dipped under the water ... and dipped ... and dipped... and swam away.

But Coyote was left sitting on the riverbank.

And do you know, even today, Coyote still has not learned to sing. He can only howl. *Ow-ow-ow-oooow!*

Snip, snap, snout,
the story is out.

What runs without feet?

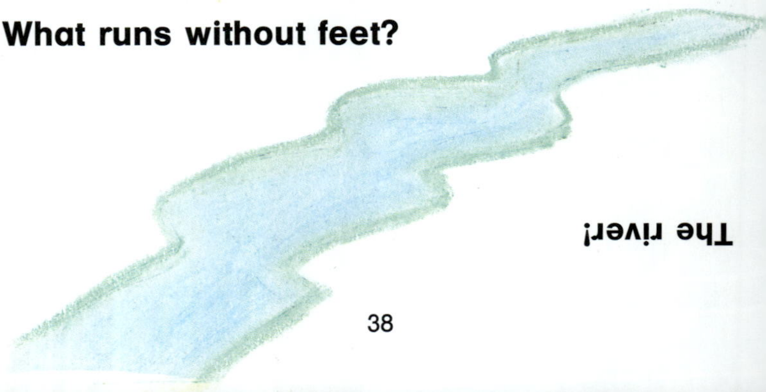

The river!

The unicorn

A wishing story from India

Once there was, and once there wasn't, a man who had a very sad life. He and his family had no money. They were very poor.

That was sad, but it was not the saddest thing. His dear old mother was blind. As she got old, her eyes got very weak until she could not see at all.

And that was sad, but it was not the saddest thing. His wife wanted to have a baby. For a long time she had wanted a baby, but no baby had been born.

And that was sad. For her, it was the saddest thing.

One day the man and the woman looked in the cupboard for something to eat, but there was no food at all.

He said, 'I will go hunting and catch something for us all to eat.'

His wife and his father watched him go out hunting. His poor blind mother listened to him go out hunting. He took his gun and he went.

He walked across the fields for a long time, but he didn't see anything he could hunt for food.

He walked by the river for a long time, but he didn't see anything he could hunt for food.

He walked in the forest for a long time, but he didn't see anything he could hunt for food.

Then he came out of the trees and into

a clearing. In the middle of the clearing was a strange animal. It looked like a beautiful white horse with a long tail and a long mane, and shaggy silver hoofs, but from the middle of its forehead grew a straight shining silver horn. It was a unicorn!

The man had never seen such a beautiful animal. He stood and looked at it for a long time. But then he thought about his mother and his father and his wife. They were at home waiting for him, waiting for him to bring back some food.

He looked at the unicorn again. It was so beautiful. But he thought to himself: 'It is still something to eat though.'

He put his gun on his shoulder and he aimed it at the unicorn. When he looked

at the unicorn along the gun, the unicorn turned and looked back at him. It seemed to be looking right into his eyes. It had such beautiful sad blue eyes that the man could not kill it. He put down his gun.

Then he heard a voice – not with his ears, but with his mind, as though the voice was talking to him inside his head.

'Thank you for saving my life. Because you did not kill me, I will give you a wish, just one wish. Whatever you wish for, it will come true. Wish well!'

And then the voice stopped, and the unicorn reared up on its back legs, and turned, and galloped away across the grass, with its long mane and tail flying behind it in the wind.

The man went home. When he came into the house his wife and his father looked at him to see what food he had brought. When they saw that he had no food they looked sad. His mother listened hard. He told them the story of the unicorn and the wish.

His mother said, 'Son, use your wish for me, so that I can see again. It is so sad to be blind and never to see the sun, or the flowers, or your face.'

His father said, 'Son, use your wish to

wish for money. Then we will never be poor and hungry again.'

His wife said, 'Husband, use your wish to wish for a baby. All these years we have wanted a baby, and now we can have one at last.'

The man looked from his mother to his father to his wife. He only had one wish. Whose wish should he choose?

He went outside and walked up and down for a short time, for a long time. He looked at the stars in the sky. What should he wish for? Whose wish should he choose? He thought and he thought and he thought.

His mother and his father and his wife waited for him in the house. At last he came inside again. They all looked at him, but nobody said anything. They waited for him to tell them his wish. The man looked from his mother to his father to his wife. Whose wish was he going to choose?

At last he spoke. He said, 'I wish my mother was looking at my baby lying in a cradle all made of gold.'

With his one wish, he had made everybody's wish come true.

His mother could see.

His wife had the baby she wanted.

And with a cradle made of gold, they would all be rich!

With that one wish, they could all live happily ever after.

I looked in the evening,
and there were many.
I got up in the morning,
and there were not any.
What are they?

The stars

These are my stories
I have given to you,
If they be sweet,
or if they be not sweet,
Take them, keep them,
or give them away.
And if you give them away,
You might tell them to someone,
Who might tell them to someone,
Who might tell them back to me again.